Praise for Tom Duga...

WIESENTH...

"CRITIC'S CHOICE"
— LA Times

"DEEPLY MOVING"
— Huffington Post

"A MUST SEE" — WABC Radio

"REMARKABLE"
— Reviewplays.com

"POWERFUL" — New York Times

"SURPRISINGLY UPLIFTING"
— Theatermania

"HAIL TO THE MENSCH!" — NY Post

"BRILLIANT" — Canadian Jewish News

"FLAWLESS" —LA WEEKLY

"THEATRICAL MAGIC" — Stage and Cinema

"NOW THAT'S THEATER WITH A CAPITAL T" — Variety

"STUNNING" — Brooklyn Daily

"SIMON WOULD KVELL" — Rabbi Marvin Hier

"TOM DUGAN IS A NATIONAL TREASURE."
— Palm Beach Around Town

"DUGAN HAS THE AUDIENCE EATING OUT OF HIS HAND."
— Florida Theatre Onstage

"WHERE TO BEGIN PRAISING TOM DUGAN?"
— Chicagocritic.com

"REALLY, DON'T MISS THIS PLAY" — Chicago Entertainment

ISBN 978-1-944068-99-8

Play Photos: Carol Rosegg
Simon Wiesenthal images graciously provided by The Wiesenthal Center of
    Tolerance
Design: Jane McWhorter

Printed in the United States of America

Published by Bashert Books Press, a division of Micro Publishing Media, Inc.
PO Box 1522
Stockbridge, MA 01262

Please contact us for bulk sales.
www.micropublishingmedia.com

Publication of this play does not imply availability for performance—
those interested should contact Tom Dugan Plays on Facebook.

"Forgiveness, this comes from God. In this world I believe in justice, in this world I believe we must address problems to prevent them from happening again."

— Simon Wiesenthal

WIESENTHAL

by Tom Dugan

DEDICATION

This book is dedicated to my beautiful wife Amy Dugan, whose unwavering love and support has sustained me for over thirty years.

— Tom Dugan

Acknowledgements

I'd like to thank my publisher Deborah Herman for holding my hand through the publishing process, The Pucci Group, for invaluable criticism and encouragement, Jenny Sullivan for her steady, creative directorial guidance, stage manager Kate Barrett for making every theater feel like home, David Hunt Stafford and Theater 40, for giving *Simon* a place to take root, my sons, Eli and Miles for lugging props around, Ray Solley and The Torrance Performing Arts Center for inviting *Wiesenthal* to the party, Shantel Dow for taking the party on the road, Daryl Roth for inviting *Wiesenthal* to the *big* party, The Wallis Annenberg Center for The Performing Arts and The Royal Manitoba Theater for kicking off our national tour, Jay Kholos for keeping the party going, Marty Rosen for his continued support and friendship, Alison Pure-Slovin for her support. Tovah Feldshuh for her support and advice. Bruce de Torres, the master of punctuation, David Cohen for legal advice and friendship, Becky and Chris Petersen for a bunch of stuff. The Opell family for having a second child.

I'd like to thank my agent, but I don't have one. I'd like to thank my therapist, I have one.

SIMON WIESENTHAL was a Polish Jewish Holocaust survivor, Nazi hunter, and writer. After WWII he dedicated his life to the search for and the legal prosecution of Nazi criminals and to the promotion of Holocaust memory and education.

About the Playwright

TOM DUGAN — Having been honored with nominations for the New York Drama Desk Award, New York Outer Critics Circle Award, Los Angeles Ovation Award, and winning the Los Angeles Drama Critics Circle Award for *Wiesenthal* produced by Daryl Roth and directed by Jenny Sullivan, *Wiesenthal* has enjoyed productions in Israel, India, Australia, Italy, and Mexico. The debut of *Tell Him It's Jackie* (introducing Kait Haire as Jackie Kennedy) was recently hailed by Los Angeles critics as "brilliant and masterful". Mr. Dugan's newest solo piece: *Tevye In New York* will premiere at The Wallis Annenberg in Beverly Hills in 2021. Mr. Dugan's other plays include *The Ghosts Of Mary Lincoln* and *Frederick Douglass In The Shadow Of Slavery.* As an actor, Tom has appeared in over 60 films, television shows and dozens of theatrical productions throughout the U.S. and Canada. For more information, contact Tom Dugan Plays on Facebook.

A Note From The Playwright

The danger for an actor performing *Wiesenthal* is to fall into the trap of playing sadness. "A sad old man telling a sad old story" sounds like an exciting evening of theater, doesn't it? Yuck! For me, the key to succeeding in this role comes from the real Simon himself, who was an amateur standup comedian before the war. Simon was a master at holding his audience's attention, mixing in some carefully placed humor with the dark lessons of what "The Human Savage" in all of us is capable of. His was a mission of hope and enthusiasm; Simon enjoyed speaking in front of people. Although I never met Simon myself, I have been introduced to dozens who knew and worked with him. Inevitably they would share a joke that Simon told them, some clean, some not so much. The man loved to laugh! That is not to say he was a silly man; when he wanted to make an important point, he spoke with the authority of the six million who had lost their voice. Simon did not guilt his audience into listening either, because he knew their attention would be short-lived. Another essential component in playing Simon well, I learned from a Holocaust survivor that I spoke with ironically named Eva Braun (Also the name of Hitler's girlfriend). After hearing the harrowing story of her life at both the Ravensbrück and Bergen-Belsen death camps – I asked her, "how in the world are you able to share these, the saddest of stories, without breaking down into tears?" Her answer set me on a course for success in the role, "I've told these stories a thousand times, whether I cry is not important, what IS important is whether or not you understand!"

FOREWORD
Martin Rosen
Simon Wiesenthal's Trusted Friend and Legal Counsel

For sixty years, Simon Wiesenthal was the world's principal voice for bringing Nazi war criminals to justice. In 1965, my good friend Herman Katz sought him out in Vienna, and soon after, we formed the Jewish Documentation Center, to support Simon's important work. (Herman died in 1975. I took over running the Center.) I am proud to have known and worked with Simon, as his lawyer, confidant, and friend, until his death in 2005. I was honored to deliver a eulogy for this great man at his funeral in Israel, along with many dignitaries.

Then one day, I was golfing with a buddy in 2013, and he told me that a one-man play about Simon was coming to Aventura, Florida. My wife Joan and I attended opening night, expecting the worst. We were immediately impressed. The way Tom Dugan captured Simon's essence was extraordinary, especially Simon's commitment to teaching young people about the atrocities of the Holocaust. No detail was overlooked. Even the set was nearly an exact replica of Simon's office in Vienna.

During the post-show Q-and-A with the audience, I introduced myself and explained my reasons for attending: one, if the show was terrible, I would do my best to shut it down, and two, if it was good, I would gladly be its biggest promotor. I told Tom that "Wiesenthal" was a fantastic tribute to Simon. At that point, Tom jumped off the stage and gave me a hug.

Since that night, Tom and I have become friends, and I have enjoyed attending many performances over the years, including the play's premiere, produced by Daryl Roth, in New York. I am incredibly grateful to Tom for using his passion and talent, through his performances and this book, to keep Simon's legacy alive, honor his work, and continue the effort to never let the six million Jews and five million others who perished in the Holocaust be forgotten.

Foreword

Alison Pure-Slovin

Simon Wiesenthal's fight against hate, bigotry, and anti-Semitism inspired my life's work long before becoming the Midwest Regional Director of The Simon Wiesenthal Center. His legacy of bringing war criminals and purveyors of hate to justice must be passed to every generation. Because, as Mr. Wiesenthal told then-President Jimmy Carter, "There is no denying that Hitler and Stalin are alive today. They are waiting for us to forget because this is what makes possible the resurrection of these two monsters."

Rabbi Marvin Hier created The Simon Wiesenthal Center to ensure that the unspeakable horrors of the Holocaust—and other injustices that followed—will never be forgotten. The Center also calls out today's acts of hate and works to prevent future occurrences from happening.

The best antidote for hate is education. In our many regional branches, The Simon Wiesenthal Center works with schools, elected officials, professionals, and community members, to teach them about racism, hatred, and anti-Semitism. From our Museum of Tolerance in Los Angeles to our countless Moriah Films productions, The Center finds, creates, and provides resources to help people confront their subconscious prejudices, see things in new ways, and deal with the hate in their communities and around the world. We want to inspire everyone, especially the young, to celebrate what we have in common, no matter our origin, traditions, or life choices, to create a world of tolerance and peace.

This is why when I was approached about the Simon Wiesenthal Center partnering with Tom Dugan's one-man play Wiesenthal, I was touched by the thoughtfulness and awareness to include our organization. This masterpiece brings to life Simon Wiesenthal and how, for nearly sixty years, he brought more than eleven hundred Nazis to justice. We share the burdens and dangers and sacrifices made by Mr. Wiesenthal and his family, as he fought for the rights of not only the Jewish victims of the Holocaust but all mistreated people.

Following many performances, I was invited to participate in audience discussions facilitated by Mr. Dugan about the play. Though most people had little previous awareness of Mr. Wiesenthal's work, the play inspired young and old to learn more and become more involved with their own communities. After these heartfelt experiences, countless people requested to volunteer, donate, and work with The Simon Wiesenthal Center.

I will always be grateful to Tom Dugan for writing this play, which helps to keep Simon Wiesenthal's legacy alive in such a visceral, effective, and transformational way.

For information about becoming involved in our work, or to make a contribution to sustain our operations, please send an email to *swcmidwest@wiesenthal.com,* or donate at Wiesenthal.com/donate.

Alison Pure-Slovin
Midwest Regional Director
The Simon Wiesenthal Center
Chicago, IL

Preface

I was watching some WWII film with my parents when I was a kid. Sometime in the early 1970s, when my mom said to me, "Your father did this, you know." I jumped and said, "Dad, you were in a movie?" "No," he said, "but I did fight in the Battle of the Bulge." That was the beginning of my education about World War II and about how my father, Frank Dugan, and thousands like him, saved the world.

Frank Dugan lower left with German prisoners 1945

He had been a foot soldier in the "Thunderbolt Across Europe," a nickname given to the 83rd Infantry of General Patton's Third Army. During his eighteen months of nearly constant engagement with the enemy, he earned the Bronze

Battle Star, and the Purple Heart, for injuries sustained during a mortar attack at the battle of St. Malo. In April 1945, his division liberated Langenstein - Zwieberge, a subcamp of the Buchenwald concentration camp system.

Feeling the 25-year-old shrapnel under his skin, I once said, "Boy, you must really hate Germans." His answer surprised me. "Nope. I don't judge people by what group they belong to. I judge them by how they behave." That didn't make sense to my 10-year-old brain, but it made an impression. Years later, reading Wiesenthal's obituary in the *Los Angeles Times* in 2005, I learned about Simon's rejection of collective guilt, and I thought, "That's what my father was trying to teach me when I was a kid."

Tom, his son Eli and his father Frank wearing a medal from the French government commemorating the WWII Battle of Normandy

It was that rejection of collective guilt that pulled me into Wiesenthal's story.

Over the course of almost sixty years, Simon Wiesenthal brought 1,100 Nazi war criminals to justice. He fought for the rights of Jewish, and Soviet, Polish, Gypsy, Jehovah's Witness, and homosexual Holocaust victims. And he defended a few German and Austrian officers who had refused to participate in "The Final Solution," rejecting, like my father, the idea of collective guilt.

As important as Simon's "Nazi Hunting" was, I believe that his greatest gift to humanity was his teaching. Through his books, lectures, and visits with countless young students at his small Jewish Documentation Center in Vienna, Simon taught us to first recognize the potential for evil in ourselves (He called it "The Human Savage"), before we can recognize it in others.

WIESENTHAL by Tom Dugan opened Off-Broadway on November 5, 2014, at The Acorn Theater. It was produced by Daryl Roth, Catherine Adler, Mr. & Mrs. Farbman, Mr. & Mrs. Towbes, and Mrs. K.L. Burns. It was directed by Jenny Sullivan; the set design was by Beowulf Boritt; the sound design was by Shane Rettig; the costume design was by Alex Jaeger; the production stage manager was Katherine Barrett; the general manager was DR Theatrical Management. The press representative was Keith Sherman & Associates.

The cast was as follows:

Simon Wiesenthal . . . . Tom Dugan
Simon Wiesenthal (understudy) . . . . .Mitch Greenberg

WIESENTHAL

A Full-Length Play for One Actor

SIMON WIESENTHAL . . . . .Human Rights Activist in his mid-90s

TIME: April 2003

PLACE : The Vienna Jewish Documentation Center, Vienna Austria

Simon Wiesenthal's Jewish Documentation Center in downtown Vienna, Austria. The walls are lined with half-empty bookshelves. Interspersed among the books are framed photographs, children's artwork, and a bathroom key attached to a rubber duck. Hanging on the wall upstage center is a large map of "Hitler's Europe." Upstage right is a door with a frosted glass window that leads into a hall. This is the sole entrance and exit to the office. Beside the door, a gray raincoat hangs on a coat rack and a prescription bottle and drinking cup rest on top of a water cooler. Up left in front of a closed window that faces the street below is a desk buried in files, books, newspapers, notepads, knick-knacks, a coffee cup, a small brown lunch bag, and a red telephone.

To the right of the desk is an armless chair. Downstage right is a loveseat with a worn comforter draped over it. Downstage left, a vase holding a single sunflower is centered on a small, low table with an armless chair next to it.

A rug sits in the center of the room. Half-packed moving boxes litter the room giving the stage a cluttered, claustrophobic feel. An energetic man in his mid-nineties steps center stage and with an Austro-Hungarian accent, he speaks to the audience in broken English.

(SIMON.)
I was sitting on a park bench not long ago when beside me sat down a wild-looking young man in a leather jacket with a nose ring and a Mohawk haircut of many different colors. When I gave him a look, the boy he said, "what's the matter, old man, haven't you ever had any fun in your life?'
"Yes," I answer. "I once made love to a peacock, and I think that you are my son."

I always like to open with a joke.

Hello, my name is Simon Wiesenthal. Welcome to the Vienna Jewish Documentation Center. I have been called "The Jewish James Bond." However, martinis give me a headache. And instead of an Aston Martin, I drive an old Peugeot. And rather than guns, lasers, and rockets, my weapons are persistence, publicity, and paperwork. One thing that 007 and I do have in common, however—overwhelming sex appeal.

I have been tracking down Nazi War Criminals for— let me see this is April 2003—so 58 years now, and in my time, I have brought 1,100 to justice. I'm not a lawyer, a detective, or a government agency. I am only a private citizen. I could have worked with one of the larger organizations, but I'm an independent kind of guy. I love people, but I don't trust them. I have written many books, traveled around the world lecturing, and have shared my passion for justice with many students right here in my office. But today, today, you are a very special group because you are—

(Sound cue: Phone rings.)

Excuse me…

(SIMON crosses upstage to the desk and answers the phone.)

Hello? Yah, Cyla, I promise you that I will be finished on time. Yes, alright, I will bring home milk. No, I won't forget. Yes, I'll write it down. I will see you at home. Goodbye, Cyla.

(SIMON hangs up and steps downstage center.)
Where was I? Yah, yah, today, today you are a very special group because…
(remembering…)
I have to bring home milk.

*(As he continues to speak, he steps back to the desk, writes on a Post-it®
note, and sticks the note on the desk lamp. He stays center stage.)*
You are not a very special group because I have to bring home milk, I bring
home milk all of the time. You are a very special group because you are my
last group.

Today, I come to the office for the final time. Yah, yah, today at five o'clock
I am retired. I will take my sunflower and walk out of that door. My wife
Cyla will be waiting at home. My daughter and the children are visiting from
Israel—they are making a party for me. Tonight my home will be filled with
the aroma of good food and the echo of children's laughter. Decorations will
be hung up only as high as little hands can reach. My wife Cyla will have one
glass of wine and kiss everyone too much. It's a beautiful picture, yes? And
yet, when I think of going home, I feel ashamed.

*(SIMON crosses down right, picks up some files from the floor and puts them
in a packing box.)*
When you wrote to me about your trip to Austria this week, and maybe you
can visit my office and ask a few questions I say,

*(He picks up the rest of the files from the floor and puts them in the other
box.)*

"No, I am finished answering questions, I am retiring. And I promised my wife Cyla I will have no more visitors."

But this morning I wake up with a problem. This morning, I'm thinking, "Well, Simon, perhaps you have answered enough questions, but isn't there one final question that you have forgotten to ask?" And so I make a call, change my "no" to "yes." And here you are. Please don't tell my wife!

(SIMON stands and crosses left.)
And so what is this one final question that Simon Wiesenthal has forgotten to ask?—I don't remember—I am only making a joke. I remember the question, but I will ask it later. (X DL) What's your hurry? You, young people, are always in such a rush, I blame the microwave. Why we not visit a little, get to know each other. First, maybe I will tell you a little a bit about myself?

Everything you hear today will be simplified. So today, you will hear Simon Wiesenthal's greatest hits. I am born in Buchach in the Austro-Hungarian monarchy. *(Sitting in chair.)* I am married. I have a daughter, grandchildren, great-grandchildren; they mean everything to me, but are of no interest to you. Of interest alone is my life in reaction to Nazism. I have survived the Holocaust, and I have tried to preserve the memory of those who did not.

Here is how this will all go—I will tell you some things that have happened in my lifetime, but there will be trouble, you won't be able to comprehend these things, these things will be beyond your power of imagination—so I will try harder and wave my arms around. This is what people do when words are not enough.

The stories of "my clients" are simple ones. *(Refers to the boxes of files.)* There'll be "the story of the bookkeeper," "the story of the chicken farmer," "the auto mechanic," "the policeman." It is not my goal today to produce tears. If that is what you want, you should go home and watch soap operas. What I wish to produce is knowledge—knowledge of the horror and an awareness of the danger.

Oops, I should show you the restroom key.

(He stands and crosses to the upstage right bookshelf and picks up the rubber duck with the key attached.)

And there are some cookies for you in the back, raspberry shortbread, yummy, a going-away present from my landlord—I've always liked him. You will excuse me one moment to make a telephone call, yes?

(SIMON speaks as he crosses behind the desk, puts on his glasses, finds the number, dials, and waits.)

There is also some coffee for you in the back.

(He sits behind the desk.)

Hello, my name is Simon Wiesenthal. *(Reading his notes.)* I'm returning the phone message from a reporter at your newspaper named Greenberg, Natalie Greenberg. She has information regarding Nazi war fugitive Alois Brunner... yes. No... no, I don't want the Obituary Department. Alois Brunner is still alive. He is the world's highest-ranking Nazi fugitive still living. Ms. Greenberg asked me to call at this time... She is not in? Will you tell her, please that Simon Wiesenthal has called her back? My telephone number is 486-4208. And to whom... Wait, wait, wait! To whom am I speaking please? "Stanley-at-the-Front-Desk."

(Writing the name down.)

Thank you so much, "Stanley-at-the-Front-Desk."

(He hangs up, takes off glasses, and stands.)

Forgive me, and so where to begin? Shame... we'll begin with shame. Shame is the most dangerous force in all human life. It is poison. Whenever people feel unworthy, empty, they will fill themselves with anything. Today this is what makes a young girl strap a bomb to herself.

After their defeat in World War I, the German people were poor, empty, ashamed. Put yourself in their place. Your child cries from hunger, and you have nothing to give her. So what do you do? Anything you can, yah?

I once saw a homeless man wearing a sign, "I will do any job?" I thought "ah hah" this is where it starts! This was his opening!

(He crosses center stage.)
Perhaps you know of whom I speak? Adolph Hitler and The National Socialist German Workers' Party—or the "Nazis." He lifted the German people's shame and dropped it right in the lap of the most popular scapegoat in history—the Jews. Whenever the majority is whipped up against the minority it is the Jews who are eventually crucified.

(He claps his hands and crosses downstage left.)
"Good news, ladies and gentleman! Forget your shame; you are blameless! The enemies are those treacherous Jews! If we get rid of the Jews, we get rid of our shame."

Now, how could any intelligent person buy that load of manure?

(He crosses center stage.)
You remember your hungry child? Hitler puts bread in her mouth; Hitler gives you a job building a superhighway. Now instead of shame, you feel pride. What is always left out of history lessons is how charismatic Hitler was. Yes. He was an amazing public speaker. He was fascinating; he was mesmerizing—you could feel heat when looking into his eyes. The German people cheered in the streets, filled with pride holding up their children. *(Mimes holding up a child.)* No longer crying from hunger, now they cry from happiness!

(He drops one arm into the Heil Hitler salute, then slowly brings his arm down.)
But this is heresy! How can Simon Wiesenthal speak this way of Adolph Hitler?
If we do not honestly try to understand how it happened then, it will happen now.

Here is some more heresy. For me, the Holocaust was not only a Jewish tragedy but a human tragedy. After the war, I urged Jews to speak not only of the six million but of the five million others killed as well; this made me unpopular.

But for me, whether it is the Christians being thrown to the lions, ethnic cleansing in Yugoslavia, or this new tragedy unfolding in Darfur, we must speak of all genocide to prevent all genocide.

Around the time of World War I, the Ottoman Empire—um—Turkey, systematically killed one-and-one-half million Armenians, and the world let them get away with it. Hitler once said, "I have no worries over killing the Jews, after all, who today speaks of the annihilation of the Armenians?"

So, why, why did Hitler hate the Jews?

There is one theory that he—*(crossing to the book on a shelf upstage left.)* may have caught syphilis from a Jewish prostitute.

(He holds the book up and then puts it back.)
But no one really knows for sure— and maybe that's not even important. What is important is that he did hate the Jews and was able to make Germany hate them too. It gave them a scapegoat for their troubles.

Before Hitler figured out the most efficient way to murder thousands of people at once, Jews were herded into a small area of a city—"ghettos." The cobblestones were pulled from the streets, so we walked in mud. A fence was built around us like a zoo. People laughed at those filthy sub-humans.

(SIMON crosses downstage right, gathers an afghan from the couch and sits.)
Well one of those filthy sub-humans was named Rosa—my mother.

From all of my memories of her was the time when I was 33 years old, and we were in ghetto in Lvov, Poland.

My mother, she prepared a little something for my young wife and I to eat and… she never eat with us, and this one day she fell, and I catch her in the air—three days she eat nothing—everything for us. This is, you know, so dramatic that more than everything else made in me this impression, only this moment, this moment… a real Jewish mother.

In ghettos, Jews were either starved or worked to death. Those who survived were eventually sent to extermination camps. There was about to be a roundup; we still had a gold watch, so I told my mother how to fix the problem. Later that day, I was allowed an urgent phone call at work.

(Light change. Throughout, the play, the light shift signifies a change from present to past and back to present as SIMON relives moments in his life.)
(As ROSA on the telephone.)
"So what have I done to deserve such a smart son as you? They took Papa's gold watch Simon and left me alone, just like you said!
Tonight, we must celebrate—can you bring home a potato?—I am making soup!!"

(Sound cue: Banging on the door.)

"One moment Simon, there is someone at the door… "

(Sound cue: Chaos at the railroad station; people cry for water in the distance.)

August 23, 1942…I am running to the railroad yard to find her. These, hundreds of people locked in these cattle cars pleading for "water, water!" I am calling out for her!

(frightened by the guards) But nothing, nothing… there is nothing, it is not a possibility to help. The next morning that train is still there. It stands in the sun for two days…

(Lights shift. Having folded the blanket, SIMON packs it in a nearby box.)

Look, now my mother would be 124 years-old. You'd think after all this time; the nightmares would stop.

I was an architect by trade, and so was of value to them. But my young wife was what they called "superfluous." However, because of her blonde hair and blue eyes, she could pass as a gentile. The last time I had seen her…

(Lights shift as we hear sounds of a train station.)

(SIMON speaks to his young wife.)
"I have fixed the problem! I have found a safe place for you! I've arranged a seat on the next passenger train out of the ghetto. No one will suspect that you are a Jew. My dear, please do not cry. Listen. Listen carefully. When you get off at the end of the line, look for the contact woman at the southwest corner of the station. She will give you a new name, and you will be safe.

My dear, please do not cry. This is happy news. I have fixed the problem. My dear, look at me, look in my eyes. Nothing has changed; nothing has changed. It is just as we promised on our wedding day… 'Where you go, I will go, where you stay I will stay.'

Now go! You will be safe in Warsaw.

(SIMON stands and steps center stage.)
Perhaps you have heard of the Warsaw uprising? Jewish Ghetto fighters in 1943 battled against the Germans for nearly a month before Nazi artillery leveled much of the city. Somewhere under that rubble lays the body of my young wife.

(To himself.)
"I have fixed the problem."

I tried to escape and was caught.

(Crosses up right to map showing the various locations.)
I was a slave laborer at the Plazow concentration camp, from there to Auschwitz, Gross-Rosen, and Buchenwald. I was a prisoner in over a dozen camps. The camps were… As punishment for looking into the eyes of a one camp guard, he had my toe cut off. There was an infection. In the spring of 1945, with gangrene in my leg, they marched us through the snow to Mauthausen in upper Austria.

Out of our original group of 6,000, only 1,000 was left. With only grass to eat, we were starving. I began losing my mind… dying…

(Lights shift as we hear the sound of a heartbeat. SIMON is leaning on the desk.)

I rest my head on a dead leg; slowly my heart begins to surrender. In my mind, I see the white stars in the heavens disappear one by one—the star of hope, the star of love, the stars of justice and tolerance, all fading away with the dying rhythm of my heart… and…

(Sound cue: The heartbeat crossfades with the sounds of approaching tanks.)

finally… the ground shakes. My heart quickens; my eyes open.

(SIMON crosses upstage right.)
Slowly, I climb over corpses to the doorway, blinded by… stars… white stars. The stars have returned? Is this a dream? Can this be true? If you can touch it, it's true. Touch the stars, Simon. Make it true, Simon.

(SIMON crosses slowly down-stage right.)
Gone is the sweet smell of burned flesh that hung in a greasy cloud over the yard.

Touch the stars, Simon. Make it true, Simon.

(Sound cue: Laughter.)

Prisoners laugh and cry into soldiers' arms.

(SIMON stumbles.)

Get off the ground, Simon. Stand up, Simon!

(Sound Cue: V.O. AMERICAN SOLDIER.It's okay, Mister, you're safe now.)

I feel his rough uniform on my skin. No words. I point…

(Sound Cue: V.O. AMERICAN SOLDIER. You want to touch the flag, Mister?)

Ya, ya, slowly, I'm helped to the American tank. With trembling hands, I reach out and make it true. I have survived.

(Light shift.)

They take away the dead. American doctors in white coats give us pills, vegetables, and meat. Not long after, I was in something called "The American War Crimes Office," where just days before the German commandant had reigned. I rub red ink on my cheeks to appear healthier so the doctors will not send me to hospital. No, no. I have to be here, this "war crimes office." It is the tip of justice!

(He sits at desk right, referring downstage right, then frightened, turns away.) These SS men are so big, so powerful, so… deadly. In their eyes, I can see the skull and crossbones. The mere thought of catching their glance makes me nauseous. It is humiliating, and for me the humiliation, the humiliation is the worst. However, standing before the Americans, these perfect specimens of the "Master Race" tremble.

I sit quietly for hours as these revolting cowards are interrogated by the soldiers. It was a slow process, but I am in no hurry. Many of the worst criminals slip through the net, but these young Americans, 21-years-old maybe, are bringing justice back into the world.

I hear one American say, "What's with the clown? He gives me the creeps."

(SIMON laughs.)
When I think of myself, a living skeleton dressed in stripes, with red-painted

cheeks, propped in the corner, a dazed little jester… the doctors weren't even sure that I would live! Many died after liberation, too far gone to be helped. Why then, why did I need to be here, in this American War Crimes Office?

I suppose I wanted to be "Exhibit A"—a living witness to the torture and killing. But more than anything else, as these "SS supermen" tremble in the face of justice.

I want them to know that I am watching. *(SIMON purposefully watches the SS man led out in cuffs.)*

These young Americans, who had fought and died to free Europe, they were like family to us.

They had seen it all; understood it all. Those who broke down the camp gates discovered the gas chambers, crematoriums, bodies piled up like wood. As long as these Americans were still around, justice is carried out.

But eventually, these men went home to their families and were replaced with others who were more interested in the frauleins than in justice.
One of these new American captains offered up to me some sage advice…

(As AMERICAN CAPTAIN, legs crossed, leaning back.)
You're a smart guy, Simon. You should know that there will always be people with different viewpoints. Try not to worry so much about it. Back home, we have Democrats and Republicans. Here you have Nazis and Jews…

I knew, in the long run, it would be our responsibility to bring these criminals to justice.

(SIMON stands and crosses center stage.)
In the early post-war months, I watched for all of these families—the millions of missing people—to come home, a great migration; walking hand-in-hand out of the forests and the countryside where they'd been hiding.

No one comes. Farmers, doctors and teachers from all across Europe—Gypsies, Soviets, Poles, Slavs, homosexuals, Jehovah's Witnesses… eleven million people who don't come home, who didn't fit into the Nazi mold of "racial purity." murdered. Six million, including all of my own relatives, executed for the sole crime of being born Jewish.

(Lost in thought for a moment, then, energized; SIMON crosses up behind the desk.)
I am making another telephone call.

(Puts on glasses, dials and stands waiting for the phone to pick up.)
Hello, "Stanley-at-the-Front-Desk?" Simon Wiesenthal calling again. I am wondering if you gave the message to Ms. Greenberg that I called… in regards to Alois Brunner, the Nazi war fugitive? Yah, yah, yah, the Nazi war fugitive. Yes, thank you, I will hold.

(Covering mouthpiece, SIMON speaks to the audience.)
While prisoners waited in line to be gassed, Alois Brunner forced them to write postcards home: "They are treating us very well in Buchenwald…" That sort of thing.

(Stepping around the desk.)
When a group of a few-hundred Jews missed a train to Auschwitz, Brunner had them herded into a boat and then sank it at sea.

Since the war, Brunner has been working for the Syrian government as a torture specialist under the name of "Georg Fisher."

Syria claims that they would "gladly" extradite him if we could only provide his exact address. From time to time, he still gives telephone interviews bragging of how he "rid the world of so much Jewish garbage."

I have…

(Back into the phone.)
Yes, yes, Stanley, I am still here. Yah, "Brunner." He is a Nazi war fugitive… I do have a pen.

(SIMON grabs a notepad and sits behind the desk.)
I should contact… Simon Wiesenthal? I am Simon Wiesenthal, Stanley.

May I please speak to Ms. Greenberg, thank you… ?

(To himself.)
What a yutz.

(To audience.)

This morning I am thinking—I do a lot of thinking this morning. Don't worry; I have not forgotten to remember "the one final question that I have forgotten to ask." But this morning, I am also thinking that, maybe on this my last day of work, I can see to it that Alois Brunner soon hears the same knock on his door that my mother heard. Maybe this I can do. Maybe if I can do this final thing, I will not be ashamed to walk out of that door.

But time is running out. Tomorrow morning my whole office is to be packed up and shipped to the Museum of Tolerance in Los Angeles. I have been working…

(Into the phone.)
Hello, Ms. Greenberg? This is Simon Wiesenthal returning your call regarding Alois… Yes, I do have a pen…

(Listening, and then writing.)
 Yah, yah… one eye and the fingers of his… left hand are missing. No, no, no he's Austrian… Were you able to take a photograph? No, no of course not… do you have the telephone… thank you… one, one, three… six? thank you so much, Ms. Greenberg… I will.

(SIMON hangs up, takes off glasses, and stands.)
Last week at the Meridian Hotel in Damascus, Syria, this journalist is exercising on a treadmill beside an elderly Austrian with an eye patch and only a thumb on his left hand. This man is Alois Brunner alias "Georg Fisher."

If I can confirm today that he is a resident of the Meridian Hotel, in the current political climate—this, this "War on Terror"—Syria may finally extradite him. But how to confirm his address?

(Crosses to the water cooler downstage right.)
My health is not what it once was, but I'm alright.

(SIMON opens the pill bottle.)
I always thought getting old would hurt more…

(SIMON takes a pill, gets an idea, then brings the bottle to his desk.)
I have mostly enjoyed good health, but I am not as invincible as I once thought I was. In December of 1945, I celebrated my liberation by riding a horse in a nearby field. Oh, it was wonderful, until the horse stops and I keep going! I break my leg. While recuperating in Linz, Austria, my friend Felix from the camps came to see me with a very odd story.

(Crosses downstage left as FELIX.)

Simon! Simon! I think I have found myself a new bride! While in Warsaw, I was looking for information regarding your wife's death. If I can help, I should help, am I right? Well, I should have known better… and I don't blame them. Everyone wants out of Poland; they see an opportunity—Leben und leben lassen. Well, three women showed up claiming to be Mrs. Wiesenthal! What can I tell you? I have traveled back here with one of them.

(As SIMON.)
Felix, my wife is dead, and what's more, you've never met her; you have no idea what she looks like. Why did you bring me this woman?

(As FELIX.)
Well Simon, this is the thing… I also lost my wife in the war, and this is a very beautiful woman; once I clear this with you, I will marry her myself! She's in the next room if you don't mind.

(SIMON turns around searching for the woman. Upon seeing her (above audience center), he is shocked. Filled with emotion he shakes his head, "No.")

(As SIMON.)
No, Felix.

(Quickly glancing over to Felix.)
… you'll have to find yourself a different bride, this one is mine.

(He crosses center stage.)
Yes, it was my young wife, Cyla. She had not died in Warsaw after all! We held each other for a long time. We shared our stories, counted the relatives we'd lost—89, and agreed it was a miracle that we had survived.

Nine months later—another miracle! Our daughter Paulinka Rose was born. And now, Paulinka has children. And her children have children! My daughter, the grandmother!

(Picking up Paulinka's framed photo, he kisses it.)

Ach! Talk about feeling old!

(SIMON gathers more photos from the shelves upstage left.)
Here is a photograph of them at the beach in Israel. If you had told me I'd live to see this, I'd have called you verrueckt.

(Sound cue: The phone rings.)

SIMON puts the framed photos in a paper bag desk left and crosses in front of the desk. Picking up the phone, he faces the audience.) Hello? Oh yes, Cyla.

(He puts his finger up to his lips in 'Shhh' gesture and turns away from the audience in secrecy.)
Yes, yes I am alone. No, no there is no group here… of course not, I promised I would have no more visitors… oh, them? *(Looking at the audience.)* It's just some friends dropping by.

(Covering the phone and whispering to the audience.)
The landlord squealed on me! That rat, I never liked him!

(Into the phone.)
Okay, Cyla. I'm very sorry. It's just one last group. I promise I will not be late to the party. Yes I'm being a good host, I've put out the cookies that the landlord gave me—yes, yes, I've always liked him… Yes, I showed them the restroom key…

(Covering the phone, he whispers to the audience.)
I showed you the restroom key, right?

(Into the phone.)
 I showed them Cyla… I showed them

(Again to the audience.)
She won't believe me. Please tell her yourself. Everyone please say, "Yah, Cyla!" I mean it. One, two, three:

(Audience responds "Yah Cyla!" into the phone.)
You see we are all very safe. Goodbye, Cyla.

(Hangs up.)
My wife worries. Women are different. Well, we've been married for 66 years, maybe she will change.

(SIMON crosses downstage right.)
A man has a suit made; he comes home and shows his wife. The wife says, "This is a terrible suit, one arm is too short, and one leg is too long. You must demand your money back!"

So the man goes back to the tailor and says, "This is a terrible suit, one arm is too short, and one leg is too long. I demand my money back!"

The tailor says, "This is a good suit. You just have bad posture. If you hold yourself as the magazine models do, relaxed and turned to the side, the arm and the leg fit perfectly."

The man thanks the tailor and walks out of the shop.

(SIMON demonstrates the awkward walk.)
As he passes two old women, one says,

(He drops the awkward pose.)
"Oh, look at the poor crippled man." The other replies, "Yes, but doesn't the suit fit nicely?"

When I'm confronted with opposition in my life—and that happens a lot—humor can be used as a bridge. People who are laughing together sometimes forget to kill each other.

(SIMON puts on his glasses, crosses to up to the left of the filing cabinet and picks out the thick "Eichmann File." He sits downstage left, and reads aloud.)
"At 8:05 p.m. on the night of May 11, 1960, a balding, middle-aged man got off the bus in Buenos Aires."

(Looks up and takes off his glasses.)
After a long day's work in the Mercedes Benz factory, Ricardo Klement was tired. He looked forward to dinner with his wife and six-year-old son. Before crossing the street, a young man politely asked for a cigarette. As Ricardo reached into his pocket, two other men jumped out. His wife never heard the screams as they sped away.

Who would do such a terrible thing? And why? Why kidnap this average man? He wasn't rich. He paid his bills. He was a good neighbor; loved his family. Ricardo Klement was an unremarkable man—apart from the fact that his real name was Adolf Eichmann *(He reveals the photo.)*

In 1942, the Nazi big wigs agreed that "the Final Solution to the Jewish Question" was mass murder. And Adolf Eichmann was put in charge. It was Eichmann who, from behind his desk, meticulously worked out the practicalities of how to kill eleven million people.

(SIMON stands and places the file and photo on the chair.)
I obsessed over the capture of Adolf Eichmann day and night for sixteen years. In Austria, I became known as "That nut case Eichmann—Wiesenthal."

My daughter Paulinka grew up with a father whose obsession with Eichmann seemed more important to him than she was. And now, all of these years later, as I sit in a Jerusalem court room, I was finally going to see the monster—a creature whose own obsession resulted in a death toll numbering well over the entire population of Austria.

(SIMON sits centerstage, looking above audience.)
The door opens and out from the very pit of hell steps…

(Lights up on the photo of Eichmann stage left.)

a bookkeeper. A timid little fellow with a twitch. A man whose vulnerability is so apparent your first impulse might be to protect him…
(confused and angry) A bookkeeper? Where is my monster? Where is the devil with the black boots and the snarling dogs? I, I, I don't want a bookkeeper. I want my monster!

After the incomprehensible bill of indictment is read—"The murder of eleven million men, woman, and children"—Eichmann simply answers…

(Sound cue: V.O. A man says "I am not guilty" in German.)

"I am not guilty."
To say this was unsatisfying would be the greatest understatement in human history.

(increasingly agitated)
It is all wrong!
This… this calmness. This normalcy.

(Lights shift as SIMON stands and crosses downstage center, exiting the courtroom.)

(Sound cue: City sounds.)

On a break outside the Israeli courtroom, the sun shines, children laugh, a train leaves on time,

(Sound cue: Giggling woman.)

a woman buys shoes! Why buy? Why buy shoes when there are millions and millions to choose from?

One-hundred truckloads of shoes
Four-hundred-thousand gold watches
Three-hundred-nineteen pounds of wedding rings.

This, this, this is a list of items collected from Treblinka, Sobibor, and Belzec in just one year! These numbers—I can't get them out of my head. How can you? How can anyone? How can the sun shine?

(SIMON screams into the street.)
Don't you care? Don't you know who's in that building?! How dare you think of other things? Life cannot just simply go on!

(Lights shift. Sounds out. A pause.)
But life does go on. Most of the people in this city have lost loved ones because of that little bookkeeper, but life does go on.

I did not capture Adolf Eichmann. An Israeli team of Mossad agents did. But in order to avoid an international incident with Argentina, the world was not allowed to know that. The search for Eichmann was a jigsaw puzzle solved with the cooperation of many different people who didn't even know each other. I'm proud to have added a few pieces.

 Eichmann's trial in front of an Israeli court in 1961 lasted fourteen weeks. He was indicted on fifteen criminal charges, including crimes against humanity itself. Eichmann explained that he was only obeying the German laws of Adolf Hitler. I believed him when he says he was not anti-Semitic.

(Directly to audience.)
How many left-handed people do we have here today? Please raise your hands… thank you. Eichmann explained that he would have just as easily gassed all left-handers if he was ordered to. And what's more, if Hitler had

instead commanded that Eichmann establish an independent Jewish state in Palestine, he would have done that! The mountain of dead human beings behind him was not due to any hatred or criminal character. Much like the 9/11 terrorists, Eichmann was not a sadist or a sociopath. It does not take a criminal mind to commit mass murder, simply blind obedience to authority.

Eichmann was convicted on all counts. His hanging on June 1, 1962, remains the only civil execution ever carried out in Israel.

(SIMON crosses left, picks up the photo of Eichmann and puts it back in the file. He sits on the front of the desk holding the file.)
And so, what was the value of the trial of Adolf Eichmann? Revenge? One life for eleven million? No. Revenge cannot be the goal. It was for me at the beginning. But I soon learned that it was justice, not vengeance, that I wanted. Because look, you cannot hate all day long. Just like you cannot eat all day; you get full. The value of the trial of Adolf Eichmann—the uncomfortable lesson for humanity was this: "If an average man is capable of such terrible things… then so am I." Humanity was forced to look into the mirror.

(SIMON places the Eichmann file on the desk and crosses behind it)
While we had the world's attention, I took the opportunity to spark interest in hunting down more Nazi fugitives. I published the book: *I Hunted Eichmann*.

(SIMON puts on his glasses and dials the phone.)
Some accused me of taking credit for the capture, which I didn't. What I did do was introduce a new word into the vocabulary of all those Nazi criminals hiding in South America—"Wiesenthal"!

(Speaking into the phone.)
Yah, yah, this is the Meridian Hotel, yes? To whom am I speaking? Zada Asmahan.

(He pronounces her name slowly, writing it down, then picks up his own prescription bottle.)
Hello, Zada. I am… Dr. Richard Kimble, calling from Austriadrugs.com. I

have a rush order for heart medication for a Mr. Georg Fisher, and I just need to verify his mailing address please… oh, you're not allowed to give out that information? I see… uh, oh… but this prescription bottle has the red sticker on it, and the red sticker means I need to rush it overnight if you know what I mean. So, if you can just quickly verify that he is a resident of the Meridian Hotel. No? Well, alright. I'll make a note.

(Pretending to write.)
Zada Asmahan said "no" to the red sticker. I'm sure Mr. Fisher's family will understand. And if not, you can explain it to them at the funeral. Oh listen, Zada, I'm sure that you will change your mind about this, and so my number is 431/486-4208. The FedEx man will be here in only a few minutes, and so I look forward to your call.

(He quickly hangs up and looks at audience.)
Not exactly Kosher, but I can live with that.

(SIMON stands and takes off his glasses.)
Now, where was I? Yeah, yeah, I published the book *I Hunted Eichmann*. I became famous overnight. Letters poured in from around the world. Those who didn't have my address simply wrote on the envelopes, "Nazi Hunter, Simon Wiesenthal" and they still arrived—evidence against camp guards, donations for the Documentation Center, and hate mail… lots of hate mail. Those letters usually began with "Dear, Jewish Dog." I still get them.

(He picks up a box with a large "M" drawn on it.)
We have a special place for them here. This is The Meshuggener File.

(He puts down the box and stands downstage left.)
My friends tell me, "Be careful, Simon."

That's like telling me to be careful on an airplane. After fastening your seatbelt, what more can you do?

Most of the threats are harmless. Some… I was out of town one night in the early '60s. At three o'clock in the morning, Cyla answered the telephone and was threatened.

(Sound cue: A WOMAN says, "Tell your husband to stop, or we will kill your daughter." Then sirens.)

Cyla suffered a heart attack.

(He crosses downstage and refers to Paulinka left, then Cyla in chair downstage right.)
The police were at the apartment when I arrived. Paulinka was frightened. Cyla was in bed, facing away from me…

(Lights shift.)

(As CYLA.)
Jews have a home. It's called Israel. Will you take us there? Adolph Hitler shot himself in the head twenty years ago. Men circle the world in spaceships now, and you can't leave 1945? Will you take us to Israel?

(CYLA stops SIMON from answering.)

Shaa! Shaa! I don't want to hear your sad stories. I don't care about your sad stories. I'm sick of them. I want to hear a happy story, Simon: "And then Mr. and Mrs. Wiesenthal took their daughter and moved to Israel and lived happily ever after!" This is the story I want to hear. Can you tell me that story, Simon?"

(Stands. As SIMON.)

No. Cyla, when we all meet in the next world, those who died in the camps will say, "Tell me what you did with this gift of life?" One will tell of becoming a doctor; another a jeweler or a banker. When they ask me, I will say, "I have never forgotten you."

The two of you I will send to Israel, but I, I cannot stop.

(SIMON crosses downstage center.)

Leaving for the office the next morning, I kissed Cyla goodbye, and she whispered, "Where you go, I will go. And where you stay, I will stay. Right here by your side."

Thank God Paulinka was never harmed… on the outside.

(Crosses left and sits.)

But I wondered about the toll the police escort, the reporters, the… separateness… was taking. When registering for elementary school, Paulinka's teacher said, "I can't believe it. I didn't know there were any Jews left!"

Before Christmas, 1953… Paulinka was seven, she came home crying… She was the only Jew in her school…

(As PAULINKA.)

What kind of people are we? All the other children visit their grandmothers, their grandfathers, their aunts, their uncles, their cousins. Why do I have no one to visit?

(As SIMON.)

What do you tell a seven-year-old? All your relatives were murdered by the parents of your classmates? Only later, very slowly, we explained what had happened. And I gave her a copy of the book *Anne Frank: The Diary of a Young Girl.* Such a gift! After reading it she say…

(As PAULINKA.)

Papa when I pray at night, is anyone listening?

(As SIMON, looking around office.)

It was my plan to stay here only a few years, and then Cyla and I would move to Israel. So, 58 years later—why did I stay in Austria? I'll tell you…

(He slaps his leg and stands.)

The skiing is excellent. Austria is a beautiful place. You've seen the travel brochures?

(Crosses to desk, picks up some papers from the down left corner of desk and reads…)

"Dear Jewish Dog…" No, that's not it.

(After tossing the letter in the "Meshuggener" file down left, he reads from a brochure while crossing downstage right.)

"Visit Austria; the magical land of Mozart and waltzes, schnitzel with strudel… " and raindrops on kittens…

(He puts the brochure on water cooler right.)

Julie Andrews sings that "The hills are alive with the sound of music…" However, those hills were alive with other things too—like perhaps a chicken farmer by the name of Franz Murer, "The Butcher of Wilna."

Wilna was known as the Jerusalem of Lithuania. It had a thriving Jewish community of scientists, philosophers, and artists. The famous violinist Jascha Heifetz came from Wilna. Eighty-thousand Jews lived there before the war. Exactly 250 were alive after the Nazis got through with them. Franz Murer was responsible for the slaughter of those 79,750 people.

In 1963, I was finally able to get that sadist into a courtroom. Murer had been enjoying a very happy life on his farm in Gaishorn. The trial was held in nearby Graz, Austria, a beautiful area… um… "The Terminator"… Arnold Schwarzenegger grew up there… "I'll be back."

I had Murer charged with seventeen counts of murder, but the trial was not going well. Murer claimed it was a case of mistaken identity. The defense attorney was very good at upsetting one witness after the next, causing them to mix up the details. And of course, in court, details are everything.

(SIMON becomes the DEFENSE ATTORNEY)

(Sound cue: Gavel pound.)

(As DEFENSE ATTORNEY.)
Let me understand this. On one hand, you say that you will never forget this day when Franz Murer threw these little babies against a brick wall. But on the other hand, you have forgotten whether this day was March 14 or March 24?

(As SIMON.)
There was one witness, however, I felt that I could truly count on. I had interviewed Jacob Brodi many years before. What struck me about him was how he had become totally detached from his emotions.

(As BRODI.)
On this morning, there were two groups of men waiting at the ghetto exit. My group was to be sent to work, my seven-year-old son Daniel's group was to be executed. When Murer wasn't watching, I waved Daniel over to my group. But Murer was watching. Franz Murer took out his revolver and shot my son in the face, here.

(Points to the right side of his face. Steps right as SIMON.)
It was a common scenario. However, his testimony was particularly valuable because of the detailed, unemotional way Jacob Brodi could tell it. Brodi, who refused to accept the restitution money West Germany began offering

in the 1950s, was living alone on a small farm in the United States. When I asked him to testify, he refused. Old emotions. He wanted to keep Pandora's Box closed. However, before entering the courtroom one morning, Jacob Brodi appeared before me. He'd heard how badly the trial was going and got on an airplane.

(As BRODI.)
I've read that Murer's two sons sit in the front row laughing and sneering at the witnesses. They will stop when I take the stand. Franz Murer killed my child before my eyes, and now *(opening his jacket)* I will kill him before the eyes of his children.

(As SIMON to audience.)
 He revealed a dagger hidden in his belt. Pandora's Box was wide open.

(Stopping BRODI from crossing left, SIMON speaks under his breath.)
Mr. Brodi, this is exactly what they want. Listen to me. No, you listen to me! The day Mauthausen was liberated, one young Jew whose baby sister was burned alive found the guard responsible. After being beaten almost to death, this bleeding SS man, lying in the mud, brandished a smile where his teeth used to be, called out to a nearby reporter "You see? Given the chance they do the same. Nazis and Jews are no different!" You understand?

(Crosses center stage.)
Jacob Brodi entered the courtroom unarmed and was the perfect witness. A few hours later, the jury returns with a verdict…

(Sound cue: V.O. JURYMAN: "In the case of Franz Murer on all seventeen counts of murder, we find the defendant 'not guilty,'"—followed by cheers and applause.)

"Not guilty." Flowers are tossed in the air. Crowds cheer in the streets. Franz Murer is a national hero.

Jacob Brodi leaves for the airport.

Why do I live in Austria? Although Austrians accounted for only eight percent of the Third Reich, half of Hitler's six million Jewish victims were killed by Austrians. They don't mention that in this travel brochure. So why have I stayed?

(He picks up the brochure from the water cooler.)
I always thought I could do more good for Israel from the outside. And if you want to find a cure for malaria, you must live among the mosquitoes.

(He drops the brochure in the trash can at desk right.)
Please don't misunderstand me. I do not believe that Austrians and Germans are "the chosen people of evil." Not at all. Look, look, look, all of my life I have rejected the idea of collective guilt. Uh oh, here comes more heresy. It is individuals that must be held to account for their actions.

Not all SS men... let me make something clear to you. There is a big difference between the rank and file German soldiers who fought a war against other soldiers—and the men of the SS who were in charge of the camps. These "heroes" fought a "war" against starvingmen, women, and children.

Having said that, not all SS men were criminals. Some, not many, but some, managed to get through the war without harming anyone.

(SIMON crosses to the bookcase left, grabs a bunch of folders, plops them on his desk, then picks out "Beck" file.)
Shortly after the war there was an SS man by the name of named Beck who was on trial. I found witnesses from Dachau confirming that he was a decent man who harmed no one. He was discharged.

(He crosses to the footstool upstage center and reaches for a framed photo.)
There was another Nazi who saved my life in the camps. Years later, I invited him to my daughter's wedding.

"But why, Simon?"

"Why?"

You tell me, what did every one of my "clients" claim at their trials? What excuse did these criminals ask humanity to accept, huh?

(SIMON waits for an answer.)
That they were "only following orders," yah? That they "had no choice," right? Wrong!!

(Holding up files.)
These two men did not "only follow orders." These two men made a choice. They said, "No!"

These are rare examples of courage that need to be pointed out

(Referring again to the boxes.)
in stark contrast to the multitude of cowards in the SS. On the other hand, not all victims were innocent. Some Jews, in order to save their own necks, did not hesitate to kill. But for me, there are no excuses: a murderer is a murderer. Nazi, Jew or Eskimo…

One morning, a man, accused of being a Jewish collaborator, burst into my office, jumped over this desk, and tried to kill me! While this lunatic slashed a butcher knife at me, do you think I said to myself, "Ohhh, the poor Jew."? No! I broke a bottle over his head! A murderer is a murderer.

I must not mix up these files, or my secretary Maggie will break a bottle over my head. *(Putting away the wedding photo, Beck and Eichmann file.)* After she drops me off at home tonight, Maggie will sweep in here like a tornado, pack up everything up, and ship it off to California. I promise I would touch nothing… except, of course, my sunflower. That I will take home.

(Referring to the sunflower in a vase downstage left.)
The sunflower has a very special meaning to me.

(Crosses downstage left and sits.)
While marching back from work detail to Mauthausen one day we passed a German cemetery. On every grave was planted a sunflower, hundreds of

them. How lucky they all were to be remembered.

We, we would be thrown into a pit and forgotten, but each of these people had their own sunflower, a sort of periscope through which the dead can receive light and love—a looking glass allowing all of those individuals to understand that they are not forgotten. This is my yahrzeit for the six million—my remembrance.

Shortly after the war, several of us volunteered to retrieve Jewish prayer books from the basement of a castle in Southern Austria. Thousands and thousands of Talmuds and Bibles intended to be exhibited in Nazi museums as relics of an extinct race.

(SIMON puts on his glasses and takes out his wallet from his jacket pocket. From the wallet, he pulls out a small piece of aged paper.)
While packing up some prayer books retrieved from an orphanage in Izieu, France, this piece of paper fell out. An eleven-year-old boy wrote, "Dear Stranger: The Germans are coming for me next. I'm the last one. But do not pity me, for now, that you've read this letter, I am no longer dead. I live in your heart. Please promise that you will never forget me. I trust you. Signed, Albert."

And so, I made a promise to remember Albert. I remember Albert by making sure his murderers don't get away with it. I remember Albert by making sure the murderers of tomorrow understand that they won't get away with it. This is how I remember Albert. And today, as I retire—give up and go home—it is Albert's words I hear: "I trust you."

(He takes off his glasses and folds up the note.)
Powerful words, "I trust you."
I don't think in my whole lifetime, I have ever said these words to another person.

(He puts the letter back.)
You are an American group, yes?

(SIMON waits for a response.)

It is appropriate; I come full circle. I have always enjoyed my friendship with America. I was visiting a college in New Jersey, and the teacher asked if anyone knew who I was. One student raised his hand and said, "Ah, yeah, you're the guy who won an Academy Award for playing Lawrence Olivier."

Olivier played me in the film *The Boys from Brazil*. Personally, I liked his *Hamlet* more than his *Wiesenthal,* but what do I know?

Hollywood has made a few films about my work. Some good; some not so good. But they all served to keep the public interest alive.

I provided information for the film *The Odessa File* starring Jon Voight and Maximilian Schell. That was a good one. Odessa was a secret Nazi organization that helped former SS men escape to South America. The antagonist in the film was based on the Nazi fugitive Eduard Roschmann who I'd been chasing for years. When moviegoers learned that he was responsible for 38,000 deaths, including 800 children, Roschmann became a wanted man. Tips on his whereabouts began pouring in from around the world.

I received a box from Bolivia. Inside was a carefully packed champagne glass and a note from a couple who thought they spotted Roschmann in a restaurant. They succeeded in getting his fingerprints on the glass. I had the prints tested—and sure enough, they were the actual fingerprints—of Maximilian Schell.

(He crosses right and pours a glass of water.)
However, after the film's release in 1974, the real Roschmann found no peace. He moved from one rented room to the next in fear of being discovered. Three years later, in a dingy flat in Paraguay, Eduard Roschmann had a massive heart attack. I am happy to have disrupted his peaceful retirement.

(He drinks.)
These Hollywood stories are uncommon. My work is not glamorous. My job is—here is how it goes: I need to find the war record of a certain German

captain. I call an office; I'm put on hold. I call a supervisor who tells me I need a permit. I apply for the permit, but it's the wrong permit. I obtain the right permit; go back to the supervisor who has been promoted. "Please talk to my assistant," I do. She informs me that I "never needed a permit in the first place— here is the information on that German captain who, by the way, died last Thursday." This is my job.

(He surveys his office.)
My office is to become a museum display, but I tell them they must show it exactly as it is.

(SIMON picks up a disposable camera from the desk.)
The important work in this life is done at messy desks.

(He takes a photo of the desk. Then points the camera at the audience and clicks.)
Say cheese!

This office is my brain. How can I say goodbye to my brain? Oh, it may not look like much, but it has worked very well for me. I know where everything is. I remember everything, including "the one final question that I have forgotten to ask."

Maybe you think I forget?

(He chuckles.)
I don't forget; it is all deliberate.

(He notices the "Stangl" file on a filing cabinet.)
That's not to say that sometimes I don't get lucky.
Laying on the floor outside of my office door one morning was a filthy looking man reeking of Schnapps. Every once in a while, you meet someone who really looks like what they are. This evil man—let's call him "Mr. Schnapps"—he had read about my search for Franz Stangl, the commandant of the Treblinka concentration camp…

(Light shift. He sits at right of desk as MR. SCHNAPPS.)

I did nothing wrong. They made me join. It's always the little guy that gets pushed around. Because of men like Stangl, little guys like us have endless trouble. After the boss finds out you were Gestapo, he fires you. It's enough to make you go back and — but I wouldn't— I mean, I didn't. I like Jews. I had a Jew girlfriend once, but you know how it is. It's all those fat cats with the money! If we could rid the world of their kind—the fat cats I mean— the Eichmanns and the Stangls you understand? *(Exhausted)* Look; I know where Franz Stangl is!

(SIMON stands, walks all the way downstage center, and waves to the audience to come closer. He whispers…)

I'll tell you a secret. My favorite thing in the whole world is not having a Nazi arrested. No, no, my greatest satisfaction in life is when one Nazi threatens the other by saying, "I will tell Simon Wiesenthal about you!" I just love that!

Mr. Schnapps continued. He offered me a special price: a penny a corpse. He wanted one cent for every person Stangl killed—700,000 lives; 700,000 pennies.

I could have snapped his filthy neck like a pencil, but finding Stangl was more important than this schmuck, and $7,000 seemed a small price to pay. Franz Stangl was working as a Volkswagen mechanic in Sao Paulo, Brazil. Stangl began his career at Hartheim Castle, a sanatorium where in the early days, the Nazis conducted experiments on "useless eaters"—the old, the mentally retarded, the terminally ill. Later this grew into wholesale slaughter using a pesticide called "Zyklon B," where hundreds could be gassed every hour.

Out of the 15,000 concentration camps across Europe Franz Stangl's Treblinka was considered "The Best." The arrival platform was painted to look like a beautiful train station there were flowers, a ticket window, first and second-class doors, but behind the façade was a storage room for human hair. Men won't burn without women. This was one of the scientific truths of Treblinka. Because of their higher fat ratio, female bodies were used as kindling.

Locating Stangl was only the beginning; it's always only the beginning. What

I do is this. I find the criminals, I find the witnesses. I turn the information over to Austria or West Germany. They extradite and put the criminal on trial. West Germany was always eager to do this, Austria was not. When they drag their feet I'd hold a press conference and shame them into action. It took three years and lots of diplomacy to get Stangl. One Brazilian politician said, "Look Mr. Wiesenthal, just send me $500 and I'll kill Stangl myself."

But it was the trial I wanted, not another dead body. Finally, in 1967, Stangl received a phone call saying that his daughter had been injured. When he arrived at hospital he was arrested by police. "Mr. Schnapps" got his money. The trial opened in Dusseldorf in 1970.

(Lights shift. Sits left as STANGL.)

I had nothing against the Jews. We only wanted their money. Even the poor had something. All that racial business—the humiliation, cruelty and hate propaganda—that was just to condition those who actually had to do the killing. But I never hated them. It was a matter of my own survival and so I went along with it. But it wasn't easy for me either. I was under a lot of pressure to produce. Firing squads began insisting on emotional duress payments, and Himmler ordered that there should be no evidence. But eventually fountains of blood began spouting from the ground. It was a logistical nightmare for me.

(SIMON stands with some difficulty, shaken by the memory.)
If I have done nothing in my life but to bring this wicked man to justice, I will not have lived in vain.

Franz Stangl was sentenced to life in prison; he died a few months later.

What I said about all of this being beyond your power of imagination…these numbers…they are hard to imagine, yes? This has been the challenge of my life, how to convey what happened when barbarism met technology. Adolf Eichmann was exactly right when he say, "One hundred dead is a catastrophe, a million a statistic." One-and-a-half-million children killed. How do you feel that?

Well, Anne Frank was one of those children, the famous fifteen-year-old girl whose diary was found on the floor of the Amsterdam house where the SS man who arrested her had thrown it. *Anne Frank: The Diary of a Young Girl* became the story of all the lost children of Europe.

Why? Because it was the story of just one girl, people could feel that. Rather than a nameless body in a mass grave, Anne Frank became your child and my child. You see the value, yes?

(Sound cue: V.O. High School Students: "Anne Frank never existed" "Jews just want more restitution money.")

During a performance of the play *The Diary of Anne Frank* in Vienna in 1958, young protesters yelled out and threw leaflets from the balcony calling the story a fraud.

I don't blame those students. I blame the parents. To cover up their own shame, they were poisoning the minds of their children, just as their minds were poisoned after World War I—remember?

Soon after the incident, I spoke with one of "the doubting boys of Europe" about Anne Frank.

(Steps right as DOUBTING BOY.)
Yeah, yeah, yeah, but there's no proof. That book's a forgery. Never happened. All those gas chambers—they were just for disinfecting clothes and the bodies, Hollywood papier-mâché. My father told me, and he was there! You're all a bunch of liars.

(SIMON crosses downstage left.)
I know what you're thinking: How could a child believe such far-fetched stories? Well think of it—which story is the more far-fetched? If someone was to tell you that your father's job was to shoot appropriately-sized Jewish children to fill potholes in an airstrip runway, would you believe it? Of course not; it's ridiculous!

It happened. No son wants to believe his father was evil, yah? How deeply do your emotions for your father go?

Now, I very much wanted to reach these "doubting boys of Europe." The only way to break this cycle of shame is to immunize these young people with the truth.

(To DOUBTING BOY.)
Young man, suppose I was to find the SS man who actually arrested Anne Frank, then would you believe?

(Steps right as DOUBTING BOY.)

Yeah, but only if he himself admitted to it, then, yeah yeah, I would have to believe.

(As SIMON.) Well, it was that simple. All I had to do now was extract a confession from a faceless, nameless functionary who arrested one of a million-and-a-half children fourteen years ago. Easy peesy.

(Crosses around desk and gets book from drawer. Puts book on desk and leafs through it.)
I had almost nothing to go on. So what? I went home and looked through my daughter's copy of the book. In the preface, the SS man who arrested the Frank family was listed as a Viennese man by the name of "Silvernagl." Unfortunately, there is no such name…

(He closes the book.)
This was the most difficult search I've ever had. What had I gotten myself into?

After all, this man was a nothing, he was a pisher. I was searching for the big names like Dr. Joseph Mengele "The Auschwitz Angel of Death," but I kept thinking of "The Doubting Boys of Europe" being poisoned by their fathers. If I could find this Silvernagl, or whatever his name was, all of the "Doubting Boys of Europe" would understand the truth of Anne Frank—and the lies of their fathers.

(He puts the book in the paper bag, desk left.)
So I went to work.

(SIMON opens a bag of grapes from his desk, eating as he paces.)
Silvernagl, Silvernagl. Let me see. He must have been of low rank since his job was only arresting people— Oh how rude of me, *(offering to the front row)* would you like a grape? No pits. Yah, it's amazing, I don't know how they do it. You need pits to make grapes; these are grapes without pits—end of grapes. Alright, Silvernagl, Silvernagl— the "V" in his name is probably really a "B," Silbernagel… which at least is a real name.

(He puts grapes on desk, crosses downstage right, pours a glass of water and drinks it.)

It was only a guess, but it was a place to start. One thing always leads to something else.

I had to be very careful; you must never accuse anyone without proof! In the 1980s, the World Jewish Congress accused the President of Austria, Kurt Waldheim, of being a Nazi war criminal— without proof!

(Replaces cup.)

So after checking the war records of all the Silbernagels from Vienna, none were stationed in Holland.

I thought about contacting Anne's father, but Otto Frank had very publicly "forgiven" the murderers of his family. I respect Mr. Frank's need to rid himself of all of that hate. But I am not interested in handing out pardons. Forgiveness— this comes from God. In this world, I believe in justice. In this world, I believe we must address problems to prevent them from happening again.

Time passed, no progress. On a plane flight, I was leafing through a copy of the 1943 Gestapo phone directory… Have you read it?

In it, I found a list of officers recruited from the Viennese police department stationed in Amsterdam! Kempin, Buschmann, Silberbauer…Silberbauer! Silvernagl/Silberbauer—maybe that's the name? If he was a policeman, maybe he still is? If he was from Vienna, maybe he still is? If he was alive, maybe he still is?

I know what you are thinking: "That's a lot of maybes." The reporter Dan Rather once asked me if I believed in miracles. I answer, "How can one be a Jew and not believe in miracles?"

Well, what can I tell you, three hundred phone calls later, Karl Silberbauer was arrested. He worked for the Vienna police department not ten minutes from this office. He confessed immediately.

(As SILBERBAUER.)
Oh yeah, I arrested Anne Frank. She was the little girl with the dark eyes. Sorry about it? Of course, I'm sorry about it. Because of her, I just lost my job.

(As SIMON.)
It made front-page news all around the world. Now all "the doubting boys of Europe" understood the truth of Anne Frank and the lies of their fathers. I think I am calling my good friend Zada one last time.

(He sits behind the desk and puts on his glasses.)
Maybe she will help me retire in peace…

(He dials the telephone and picks up the prescription bottle.)
Hello Zada, Dr. Richard Kimble calling again. I'm wondering if you have maybe changed your mind…

(He listens.)
No? Still no? The red sticker has not impressed you, huh? I really thought I had something there.

(Takes glasses off.)
Look, you sound like an intelligent woman, Zada; perhaps you suspect that I am not telling you the truth, yes?

(He listens.)
Yah, my real name is Simon Wiesenthal. And Mr. Fisher's real name is Alois Brunner. He is a Nazi war criminal. Nazi… from World War II?

(He listens.)
I realize that you are very busy, but I am only needing you to confirm that he is a resident of the Meridian Hotel...

(He listens again.)
I cannot call you tomorrow. There are no more tomorrows. Won't you help me, Zada?

(He listens.)

You "don't want to get involved?" I understand. But listen. Legally, all I need is for an employee of the Meridian Hotel to confirm, in writing, that he is a resident…

(He listens.)

No, no Zada… wait, wait, wait…

"A sweet old man?"

Let me tell you something, Zada. Sixty-one years ago, this very day, that sweet old man marched 345 children out of an orphanage in Izieu, France, and shot them in the head.

(SIMON quickly takes out his wallet to retrieve the "Albert" letter. He reads quickly.)

I carry a letter here from one of those children I will read it to you: Dear Stranger, the Germans are coming for me next…"

(ZADA cuts him off.)

But perhaps it is your business, Zada. Perhaps it is all of our business, huh? Do you have children, Zada? Aw, what are their names?

Please think it over, and if you change your mind I will be here for only a few more minutes, and so I look forward to your—

(ZADA has hung up. SIMON then hangs up the phone and takes his glasses off. He is fatigued. He carefully returns the letter to his wallet and puts his wallet back into his jacket.)
And so it goes…

(SIMON glances left to the sunflower, then turns his attention back to the visitors/audience.)
Can we be honest here? You come here today to see a museum piece, yah? A kindly old grandpa, maybe someone tells you that I am a hero? Yes, yes, yes, heroes are very comforting. Heroes fix the problem!

I have in this room the names of 22,000 criminals. I catch 1,100— that is 5 percent. Five percent! I am ashamed of this number. I think that maybe yes, I am a hero. I am a five percent hero.

(Referring to packing boxes filled with awards.)
 I have here many awards: Congressional Medal of Honor, The French Legion of Honor, Knight of the British Empire. I would give them all back, every last ribbon, plaque, and citation if that woman would simply call me back.

There has been progress. But I have not "fixed the problem." I have not "fixed the problem!" The human savage still lurks just below this wafer-thin veil of civilization. You call him Hitler or Stalin, Mao Zedong, Kaddafi, or Bin Laden; he will always be a part of us. All we can do is contain him.

(Sound cue: Car horn.)

Oh, my secretary, Maggie has come for me!
(SIMON crosses to the window. He opens the window and waves down at MAGGIE, then closes the window.)

Oh, maybe just a few more minutes I…

(Looking at the phone, SIMON stands still for a moment, then…)
No. My time here is finished. My wife Cyla is waiting at home, waiting at our front door for me to finally come home from the war.

(SIMON crosses up right, puts on his coat, picks up his beret, then suddenly…)
Remember milk! Ah hah!

(He picks up the "milk" Post-It® from the lamp and sticks it to his coat and puts his grapes and pill bottle into a paper bag and picks up the bag.)
Won't you see yourself out? Please you take the cookies with you, turn off the lights and…

(SIMON retrieves the sunflower from the vase.)
There is a belief in Judaism that by remembering the dead, we keep them alive. But it is not for themselves that they need to be remembered… it is for you. And so here is the one final question that Simon Wiesenthal has forgotten to ask. After I am gone… who will remember Albert?

(SIMON gives a slight bow and begins to exit with paper bag in one hand and the sunflower in the other. He stops. Putting the sunflower on the chair just right of the desk facing the audience, he looks happily at them and then…)
I trust you.

(Satisfied, SIMON puts on his beret, and with the paper bag in hand, exits through the door upstage right. The lights fade into a single spotlight on the sunflower center.stage. Lights fade out.)

THE END

TALK BACK

After many performances, there is time for the audience to ask questions of the playwright and actor. This question-and-answer period is called a talkback. In a one-man show, that is typically just me. I was fortunate to meet Marty Rosen, Simon Wiesenthal's close friend, legal counsel, and confidente, who joined me for several talkbacks.

Each audience differed and added a profound element to my connection to the play and my role as Wiesenthal. The following is a sampling of the kinds of questions they asked.

Why did you write this play?
My father's stories of the war significantly influenced my thinking, partic-ularly his perspective of the aftermath. My father was a very compassionate and tolerant man, and I kept that in mind as I worked on this play. I saw similarities between Simon Wiesenthal's philosophies and those taught to

me by my father. People ask me if I am Jewish because of the play, and they are surprised when I tell them I am not. I am Irish Catholic, born and raised in New Jersey. Writing about Wiesenthal resonated with me because of the important lessons my father taught me and because my wife, Amy, and our boys, Eli and Miles, are Jewish. Tolerance plays a big part in my life, and teaching the value of tolerance was, I believe, Simon Wiesenthal's greatest achievement.

Another more personal reason was I believe the WWII generation did a great job passing down to my generation the valuable lessons learned from the Holocaust. I felt that it was incumbent upon me to pass those lessons down to later generations. Writing and performing Wiesenthal is my way of doing that. I am also mindful that my sons are watching me. When they look back at what their father did with his life, I want them to feel proud.

How long did it take you to write this play, and was it hard to study such a dark subject?

It took about three years, two for research and one for writing, and it was hard. At one point, it overwhelmed me. I sat on the floor and held my two Jewish sons, and I just felt so grateful that they were born in the U.S. during this century. I learned a big lesson watching a documentary about Auschwitz. An eyewitness described seeing Dr. Joseph Mengele do something so revolting; I went into a sort of shock. I had missed the next ten minutes of the film before I realized what had happened. My mind—to protect itself from the excruciating image—just went numb. This experience taught me that as a playwright, I had to find a way to convey the horrors of the Holocaust while keeping the audience engaged.

Does playing this part take an emotional toll on you as an actor?

I'll answer that with a story. I was at a jazz club with a friend years ago, and the great Blues singer Sarah Vaughn made a surprise appearance; she was spectacular- not a dry eye in the house. After the set, I asked her if singing the blues brings her down? She said, "oh no, singing to all you folks squeezes that sadness right out of my heavy heart. I pour it all into the songs, and now I feel lighter, happier. And if I'm really doing my job right, maybe the audience feels lighter, and happier too.

Have any Holocaust deniers come to the play?

Not that I know of. One night in a Beverly Hills theater, during a talkback, a young woman asked, "Is this all true?" She had been told, while growing up, that the Holocaust was nothing but a big exaggeration. I calmly explained to her about my intensive research, how I had interviewed survivors, and that all of the numbers and stories in the play had been triple-checked for accuracy. Then I asked her why did she think, her parents would teach her such a lie. Tears came down her face as she said that her great-grandfather was Adolf Eichmann, the "architect" of the Holocaust, the biggest murderer in history. It was a fascinating night at the theater because the audience and I were confronted with the temptation to feel, assign collective guilt, and judge her for what he did. But she was guilty of ignorance only (if "guilty" is the right word). I gave her a lot of credit for asking a brave question and identifying herself in that room full of strangers.

Was Albert real?

Albert was an 11-year-old boy on the list of children murdered in 1944 by the Nazis at an orphanage in Izieu, France. The letter itself is a compilation of written sentiments left by three different Holocaust victims, secretly written in prayer books, found after the war.

"I wonder if I would have been strong enough to stand up against the Nazis?" asked one student. I was happy to have an answer, as Simon himself was once asked the same question. (I paraphrase) "I can absolutely answer that question. Hitler and the Nazis did not simply fall from the sky as a superior military force ready to dominate the world. The so-called Third Reich was built over time, one small injustice on top of the next. I will answer your question with a question. How do you respond to injustice in your life today? Do you ignore it, shrug it off, turn the other way? Or do you speak out against it, stand up to those who threaten and cheat? How you behave now is how you would have behaved then."

"Why hate?" one young man asked. The simplicity and purity of his question took me aback. Here is the answer I gave that student, and I hope it was sufficient. "The father loses his job. He feels ashamed and weak. The father goes home, and he bullies his son, which makes him feel powerful

and strong. Now the son feels ashamed and weak. The son goes to school and bullies his classmate, which makes the son feel powerful and strong. The more classmates he bullies, the more powerful and strong he feels. If no one challenges the son, the pattern continues. Soon the son has a growing gang who bully the class, then the school, then the town, country, and the world."

What interesting people have you met while touring Wiesenthal?

After one of my Off-Broadway performances, a shy older man was pushed to meet me by his wife. "I enjoyed the show" was all he got out before his wife said, loudly, "He caught Eichmann!" It was true. He was Moshe Tavor, one of the team of men who captured Eichmann in Argentina in 1960 and brought him to Israel for trial. I also met three generations of Anne Frank's family: her cousin Monica Smith (90s), Monica's daughter Nicole (40s), and her daughter, an Anne Frank look-alike, Sophie (15, the same age as Anne when she died).

Tom and Monica Smith, Anne Frank's cousin

❖ ❖ ❖

After the curtain call at The Wallis Annenberg Theater in Beverly Hills, Rabbi Marvin Hier (The founder and dean of The Simon Wiesenthal Center) sprang to the stage. While shaking my hand, he said, "Simon would kvell!".

I ran into journalist Ted Koppel, who was doing a book signing in a theater next door. When I told him that I was performing a one-man play about Simon Wiesenthal, he asked 'Why?" I told him that I thought Simon's lesson of tolerance was a worthy subject. With a wry smile, Koppel replied, "I always thought he was a pain in the ass." I'm sure he was. When it came to getting his message out into the media, Simon was a force of nature.

BEHIND THE SCENES

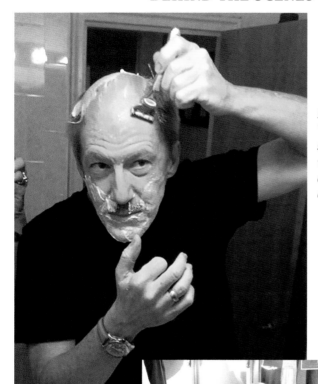

Preparing to play Simon Wiesenthal included shaving my head, wearing a fat suit, and an hour of make up every night.

My dressing room at the Acorn Theater on 42nd St. with my sons Miles (11 yrs. with glasses) and Eli (13 yrs.). My sons enjoyed watching me prepare by applying an hour's worth of makeup.

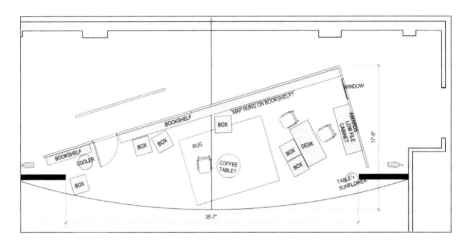

*An early set design (above), and the finished New York set by Beowulf Boritt.
Those who knew Simon say that his real office was even messier.*

OPENING NIGHT

The Playbills Arriving at the Acorn Theater.

Opening night in New York, with my wife Amy Dugan.

Tony Award-Winning playwright Tony Kushner with producer Daryl Roth Opening night New York November 5, 2014.

Dinner at Sardis in New York with trusted stage manager Katherine Barrett, we've done over 500 Wiesenthal performance together.

With Director Jenny Sullivan.

Wiesenthal understudy Broadway veteran Mitch Greenberg, me, Jerry and Amy Stiller, NY.

Actor/playwright George Takei after a Wiesenthal performance, his musical Allegiance (about life in a U.S. Japanese internment camp) was soon to open on Broadway.

Opening night party with famed sex therapist and Holocaust survivor Dr. Ruth Westheimer. (She asked my wife Amy's permission before she gave me a kiss.)

The New York reviews 2014

Many young people have dreams of becoming actors or writers. This man, Fred Ruggiero, my 9th grade drama teacher inspired me and was there to share my opening night and wait for the reviews.

Tom and Tovah Feldshuh at the commemoration of the 76th Anniversary of kristallnacht "the night of broken glass." November 10, 1938 was a day of coordinated destruction when more than 1,000 Synagogues were destroyed and German Jews were chased, terrorized and many were killed.

On tour in Georgia with stage manager Kate Barrett, visiting with Rosalynn, and President Jimmy Carter who awarded Wiesenthal a Special Congressional Gold Medal in 1980.

ABOUT SIMON WIESENTHAL

Simon Wiesenthal first came into prominence for his role in tracking down Adolf Eichmann, who was the major logistics person for Hitler's "Final Solution of the Jewish question." Eichmann organized the mass deportation of the Jews to ghettos and extermination camps. Vienna's papers dubbed Wiesenthal der Eichmann-Jäger,—the Eichmann-hunter—for his role in helping the Israeli government track down Eichmann in Argentina. On May 11, 1960, Mossad captured Eichmann, who was tried in Jerusalem and executed by hanging.

Simon Wiesenthal survived the Holocaust after being deported from his native Poland. He was finally liberated from the Mauthausen death camp in Austria in May 1945. Wiesenthal believed his wife, Cyla, had perished in the camps, but the two were miraculously reunited after the war. Between the two, they lost 89 family members to the Nazi's senseless murder of Jews and other "undesirables."

Wiesenthal and his wife Cyla, shortly before WW II.

After liberation, in 1945, Wiesenthal volunteered to work for the United States Army to help locate war criminals in Austria. Then he was employed by the U.S. Office of Strategic Services and the Counter-Intelligence Corps. In 1947, with volunteers, he opened a small Documentation Center to help Jews trace missing relatives. At the same time, he began tracing other Nazi criminals who were still at large. The location of Eichmann was significant to his work because public sentiment to pursue justice was waning. The international publicity about Wiesenthal's role in Eichmann's capture renewed interest in the cause. He continued to dedicate his life to the pursuit of Nazis until, to his knowledge, he had outlived them.

When asked why he dedicated his life after the war to the relentless pursuit of Nazi war criminals, he replied, "When we come to the other world and meet the millions of Jews who died in the camps, and they ask us, 'What have you done?' there will be many answers. You will say, 'I became a jeweler.' Another will say, 'I smuggled coffee and American cigarettes.' Still, another will say, 'I built houses,' but I will say, 'I didn't forget you.'

Wiesenthal was 33 and an architect and engineer living in Galicia, Poland, now Ukraine, when he was captured and put in a concentration camp. His career made him useful to his oppressors, so he was then sent into forced labor. His wife, Cyla, was blond, which may have helped spare her. Between 1941 and 1945, he was imprisoned in over 12 concentration camps.

Wiesenthal witnessed unimaginable atrocities, including watching his mother being shoved into a cattle car destined for extermination. At one point, he escaped but was recaptured and, fearing torture, twice tried to take his own life. He believed in the idea of bashert, a type of destiny that instilled a great sense of purpose and meaning for his life after the war.

When the Americans liberated Wiesenthal, he weighed only 97 pounds. He returned to Vienna to set up his office; even though he could have gone to Israel or the United States, he chose to stay in the heart of the places responsible for the crimes. He set out to create a persona that would strike fear in his targets as a relentless justice-seeking machine who would never stop.

Wiesenthal made it clear many times that he did not have revenge as the motive for his work. His goal was to teach new generations about the truth. As we can see in the years since his death in 2005 at the age of 96, hate groups and those who wish to forget, downplay the extent of these historical events. On some level, Wiesenthal's understanding of human nature caused him to create a legacy that would assure the factual proof that these horrors truly happened and could happen again if people are not vigilant.

His work continues through people dedicated to carrying on his legacy. He said if we do not teach the next generation, "The schools would fail through their silence, the church through its forgiveness and the home through the denials or the silence of parents. The new generation has to hear what the older generation refuses to tell it."

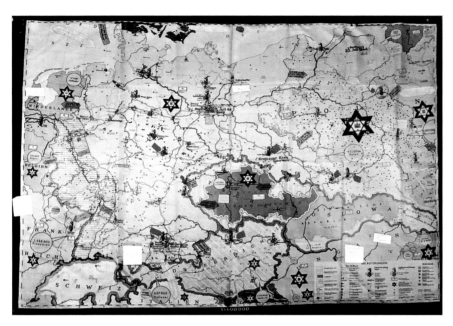

*We used an exact replica of Simon's map of Hitler's Germany
for the New York production.*

Wiesenthal often spoke about families who wanted peace in their little nests. While understandable, this leads to apathy. When people do not see crimes against humanity as relevant to their lives, criminals can once again

The dean and founder of the Simon Wiesenthal Center, Museum of Tolerance and Moriah Films, Rabbi Marvin Hier, with Simon at his Vienna office in the 1990s. Both men loved to laugh.

rise to power. He describes the rise of Nazism as, "criminals climbed to power and kept it. The Holocaust did not happen overnight. It was a systematic division of people and a choreographed strategy of propaganda. Hitler found the people's vulnerabilities and fed them solutions." His message is that in any generation, all people can be at risk.

Wiesenthal once said, "For me, the Holocaust was not only a Jewish tragedy but also a human tragedy. After the war, when I saw that the Jews were talking about the tragedy of six million Jews, I sent letters to Jewish organizations asking them to talk also about the millions of others who were persecuted with us together —many of them only because they helped Jews."

Not only was Wiesenthal concerned that people acknowledge all those lost to the Holocaust, he believed that it was important for all people to see these events as relevant to themselves. Only with the understanding that anyone can fall victim to tyranny can something like this be prevented. In his book, *Every Day Remembrance Day: A Chronicle of Jewish Martyrdom*, Wiesenthal shows that on every day of the week and in every generation, Jews have been persecuted and scapegoated. He wanted to educate people of all societies to beware of human rights violations. Anyone can become a victim when no one is paying attention.

Simon at The Carter White House accepting a Special Congressional Medal of honor in 1980.

At the Whitehouse ceremony with Martin Rosen, Simon's lawyer and best friend, 1980.

Simon Wiesenthal is relevant today because his message is that to remember history is to prevent crimes from happening again. History will repeat itself unless humanity learns the lessons. He believed having information is a defense, so he set about educating as many people as would listen. In other words, "If you know from history the danger, then part of the danger is over because it may not take you by surprise as it did our ancestors."

Wiesenthal also firmly believed that even the worst of the criminals were not born that way. Someone had to teach them to hate. Whoever, or whatever causes people to hate others only because their race or religion, society can prevent the magnitude of the events of that dark period of history and other genocides before and since, with acute awareness and education.

Wiesenthal could not have fully anticipated the explosion of social media and instantaneous information. However, he was a witness to the worst crimes against humanity. He saw the potential for technology to be used as a tool for propaganda and indoctrination. When he died in 2005, he passed the torch to future generations to be critical thinkers and human beings who care for each other.

In every generation, someone rises to destroy the Jews. Perhaps it is because the Torah beseeches Jews to be a light amongst the nations. Simon

Wiesenthal knew there must always be Jews, even if to be the proverbial canaries in the coal mine, to warn of the first sign of potential danger.

"There will always be Jews as long as they remember. There is no greater sin than to forget," he said.

Wiesenthal begins his book *Every Day Remembrance Day* with this story:

In 1942 when the Jewish poet Layser Aychenrand escaped from the deportation train to Auschwitz and reached Annemasse on the Swiss border without documents, the customs officer questioning him asked his age. He answered: "I am two thousand years old…"

BOOK CLUB QUESTIONS

◆ What did you like best about this play?

◆ What did you like least?

◆ Share a favorite quote from the play. Why did this quote stand out?

◆ What feelings did the play evoke for you?

◆ If you got the chance to ask the author of this play one question, what would it be?

◆ If you got the chance to ask Simon Wiesenthal one question, what would it be?

◆ What surprised you about the story?

◆ What was unexpected?

◆ What did you learn about this play's subject?

◆ What aspects of Wiesenthal's story could you most relate to?

Simon Wiesenthal
1908-2005

STUDY GUIDE FOR STUDENTS

Teaching about the Holocaust is a necessary challenge. Aside from its historical importance, the lessons of this tragic and horrific event transcend the period during which it occurred. Young people today face unprecedented access to information but also questionable influences. Critical thinking about the world around them is a skill that is vital to a safe, sane society.

We have broken up the study guide into topics that can encourage further discussion. Our hope is for students to see the broader relevance of the play and the subject matter. Teaching about the Holocaust raises many sensitive concerns. Shoah is the Hebrew word for catastrophe. Each year, on the 27th day of the Hebrew month of Nisan, people worldwide remember the Holocaust. The day is called Yom HaShoah Holocaust Remembrance Day, an opportunity for classroom study as there are related events in most communities. Some schools limit the historical study to the upper grades. Many schools throughout the world are teaching lessons about the Holocaust as early as elementary school. Teachers find It is never too early to encourage children to accept diversity and differences among their peers and show empathy and compassion. The following questions can be a starting point to discuss all marginalized people, racism, sexism, prejudice, and even bullying.

THE HOLOCAUST

Simon Wiesenthal often said that the horrors of the Holocaust began with the Jewish people but was not limited to them. Between 1933 and 1945, the Nazis and their collaborators systematically murdered six million Jews. Also, they murdered millions of non-Jews for reasons of politics, disabilities, homosexuality, race, or for helping Jews.

- Why do you believe Simon Wiesenthal dedicated his life to the pursuit of Nazis?

WIESENTHAL

- What is your reaction to the play, Wiesenthal?

- Did you learn anything you hadn't already known?

- The following quotes are by Simon Wiesental. What do they mean?

"The History of man is the History of crimes, and History can repeat. Information is a defense. Through this we can build, we must build, a defense against repetition."

"Freedom is not a gift from heaven… One must fight for it every day."

"Survival is a privilege that entails obligations. I am forever asking myself what I can do for those who have not survived."

TECHNOLOGY

Simon Wiesenthal once said: *"The combination of hatred and technology is the greatest danger threatening mankind."*

- Do you agree or disagree?

- If the internet had existed during the years 1933 to 1945 as it does today, how would it have influenced the Holocaust?

- Would it have been a good thing or a bad thing?

- Could it have prevented the tragedy, or would it have made it worse?

- How is technology misused today?

- What are the good uses of technology?

CULTS

- What are cults?

- Are cults related to Nazism?

- How are cults formed?

- Can the Nazis be considered a cult? How?

- How do hate groups recruit new followers?

- What methods do they use to target their enemies?

- Research one or more cults and compare them to the Nazis.
- What lessons can be learned about how they start?

TOLERANCE

- The Wiesenthal Center is called the Museum of Tolerance. Why?
- What examples of intolerance can be found in American History?
- What are some contemporary examples of intolerance?
- How can intolerance, discrimination, and prejudice be prevented in today's world?
- Have you ever been the victim of intolerance?
- Have you been intolerant of others?
- Why?
- How can you make a positive difference to prevent the spreading of hate and intolerance against any group of people?

HATE GROUPS

In an interview, when asked if he was retiring, Simon Wiesenthal explained that he might not be searching for more Nazis, but that doesn't mean that no more will come his way.

"From time to time, we may wish to find someone." He says another part of the work is of increasing importance—documenting the rise of the neo-Nazis and historical revisionists. "There are now small groups in Germany and Austria who say not everything about Nazism was bad. And one day when the situation is good for them, these small groups could grow into a bigger group of neo-Nazis." https://www.theguardian.com/education/2001/oct/29/socialsciences.highereducation

- Are there contemporary hate groups growing throughout the world?
- What do they say about Nazism?
- What is Holocaust revisionism?
- What do the revisionists claim about the Holocaust?
- What information do they use to back up their claims?

- How do they reach their audience?

- Are they all fringe members of society, or has this thought process reached the mainstream in certain parts of the world?

VOCABULARY WORDS AND PHRASES
TO DEFINE AND DISCUSS

- *Antisemitism*

- *Civil Rights*

- *The Civil Rights Movement*

- *Discrimination*

- *Gender Discrimination*

- *Genocide*

- *Ghetto*

- *Hate Crime*

- *Intolerance*

- *Racism*

- *Prejudice*

- *Propaganda*

- *Tolerance*

- *Scapegoat*

We are always interested in how students respond to these questions and if the play impacted them in any way. We encourage teachers to reach out to us via our website: www.bashertbookspress.com

NOTES